Pathways

Finding God in the

Present Moment

JEAN MAALOUF

ACTA

ASSISTING CHRISTIANS TO ACT

PUBLICATIONS

Pathways
Finding God in the Present Moment
by Jean Maalouf, Ph.D.

Jean Maalouf has two doctorates from the Paris-Sorbonne University in France. He presently lives and works in New Milford, Connecticut.

Edited by Gregory F. Augustine Pierce
Cover design and photo by Tom A. Wright
Page design and typesetting by Barbara J. Garrison

Scripture quotations are from the *New Revised Standard Version* of the Bible, copyright (c) 1989 by the Division of Christian Education of the National Council of the Churches of Christ in the U.S.A. Used with permission. All rights reserved.

Copyright © 2000 by Jean Maalouf

Published by: ACTA Publications
            Assisting Christians To Act
            4848 N. Clark Street
            Chicago, IL 60640-4711
            800-397-2282

Library of Congress Catalog Number: 00-106102
ISBN: 0-87946-215-9
Year: 04 03 02 01 00
Printing 8 7 6 5 4 3 2 1 First Printing
Printed in the United States of America

CONTENTS

DEDICATION

To all those who explore the
myriad pathways to God in the
simplicity and wonder of the
present moment.

INTRODUCTION

When I travel, I usually know where I am going, why I am taking the trip, and what I want to do and see. I do all the necessary homework before I go. Most of the time, the trip provides me with all that I am expecting.

This time, however, I decided to do something different. I said to myself, "Write a book without any preconceived notions of what it will be about." No clear destination was chosen, no goal was determined ahead of time, no agenda was established. I left for an unknown destination, and *Pathways* was the result.

It has been a beautiful, although sometimes very painful, experience for me to write this book. I have learned much about life and my own spiritual motivations. I have shed many tears and enjoyed many laughs in the process.

The two texts of Scripture that came to my mind as I wrote were: "Go from your country and your kindred and your father's house to the land that I will show you" (Genesis 12:1) and "Abraham obeyed when he was called to set out for a place that he was to receive as an inheritance; and he set out, not knowing where he was going" (Hebrews 11:8).

No map and no name of the destination were provided me for this sacred journey. I was to pick my own pathways where none existed.

This is not how I normally live my life. I've learned the necessity of having an agenda, a goal, a schedule. I believe in the importance of being on time at the right place. I pride myself in being focused, disciplined, determined and organized. I believe in setting goals and reaching them. I've never paid much attention to the "getting there" process. The journey itself has always been a means to an end, not an end in itself.

Abraham, the great Hebrew patriarch, did not live this way. He was interested in the journey itself, and he did not seem to care about where he was going. He trusted the God who told him to go, and this trust was enough to sustain him.

How silly all my planning and attempts to control the outcome now seem. I just did not trust God enough. Even though Jesus promised that he is "the way, and the truth, and the life" (John 14:6) and issued the invitation to "come, follow me" (Mark 10:21), I still thought that I needed to come up with a spiritual map that showed exactly where I was headed.

Frankly, I've never fully trusted God, even though I've always said that I did. I never trusted without trying to impose my own demands, expectations, conditions, reservations. When I did claim to trust God, it was in order to keep my distance from real life and having to struggle with its uncertainties, complexities and aggravations.

To write this book, however, I had to trust God in spite of my fears. I discovered that one of the best places to find God is in the present moment. I learned to decipher God's footprints on the sidewalks of my life. They were always there, but I did not know it.

For most of my life, I thought that God was interested in the "big picture" only. I did not realize that each obvious step in my life's journey was also a step in my spiritual development. Now I know that my life is a spiritual journey from morning to evening, from job to job, from one encounter with others to the next, and that everything I do or am can be a pathway to the divine.

In order to write this book, I had to give up destinations, agendas and maps. God was in control, and each topic, each insight, each chapter took me somewhere I've never been before. I let God lead the way—not by a passive resignation nor by a fatalistic attitude that "whatever comes is fine" but by turning actively and with complete awareness to the Spirit that is always moving inside of me.

I had begun with plans to change *the* world, but I realized that what I really needed to do first was to change *my* world and to recognize—totally and without reservation—that God is in every aspect of it.

So, if this little book is helpful to you, it will be because you do not expect too much from it. It is an unscheduled trip, without any clear destination or itinerary. It is a sacred journey to discover the pathways to God that are part of every present moment.

One

PRESENCE

"It is the Lord!" (John 21:7) the beloved disciple exclaimed when he met Jesus on the shore after the Resurrection. "It is the Lord!" is also what we should say each moment of our lives.

Our presence to ourselves and to each other is the best way we have to live fully, to love others, to be our truest selves. Wherever we are and whatever we happen to be doing at any given time is our most direct path to God. God's action in us does not come in a past tense, nor in a future tense, but in the present tense—right here and right now.

Most of us are ordinary people, are we not? We have work to do, food to prepare, deadlines to meet, appointments to keep, many important or trivial decisions to make. Our lives are filled with pleasant and not-so-pleasant events, successes and disappointments, and episodes of both sadness and joy. We should welcome all these things into our lives as the expression of the presence of God in the world. This welcoming of the grace of the present moment is what holiness really means.

Jean-Pierre de Caussade, the author of *Abandonment to Divine Providence,* tells us: "God speaks to every individual through what happens to them moment by moment." The action of God is always present, revealing itself in our lives in the most tangible manner. But can we realistically live every moment without any reference to the past and to the future? Don't we have roots in the past and plans for the future?

Wherever we are and whatever we happen to be doing at any given time is our most direct path to God.

Indeed, the past and the future have considerable influence on the way we live the present moment. However, the past and the future mean nothing if they are considered in themselves without reference to the present. What is real is the present moment—not the past, which is gone, nor the future, which is a dream. The Christian is supposed to be a person of the present moment, not enjoying it in an "eat-drink-and-be-merry" sense but living it as a gift from God and using it as the very path to God.

The best way to live the present moment is to abandon ourselves to divine providence. In this act of abandonment, we discover faith, hope, love, trust and confidence. The present moment becomes filled with the infinity and intensity of God, and our compliance to God's will becomes the natural thing to do.

When Jesus wanted to make this point clear to his disciples, "He called a child, whom he put among them, and said, 'Truly I tell you, unless you change and become like children, you will never enter the kingdom of heaven" (Matthew 18:2-3). On another occasion, he again proposed children as models for Christian spirituality: "Let the little children come to me, and do not stop them; for it is to such as these that the kingdom of heaven belongs" (Matthew 19:14).

Children are spiritual models precisely because of their ability to trust without the slightest reservation. This sense of abandonment to God was the whole basis of Saint Therese of Lisieux's "Little Way" in her autobiography, *Story of a Soul:* "If I did not simply live from one moment to the next, it would be impossible for me to keep my patience. I can see only the present, I forget the past, and I take good care not to think about the future. We get discouraged and feel despair because we brood about the past and the future. It is such folly to pass one's time fretting, instead of resting quietly on the heart of Jesus."

Are we sensitive enough to the present moment to perceive God's ongoing action in our lives? Are we able to detect God not only in the beautiful and wonderful things that happen to us, but also in the misfortunes, the disasters, the painful circumstances, the disorders, and the trivialities?

When we recognize God in the present moment, it becomes eternal— transcending any past or future moment to become completely intense, passionate and meaningful.

Even the "divine darkness" of the mystics is there to remind us of the various ways that God pulls us closer.

Jesus did not do away with suffering, nor did he explain it or justify it. Instead, he taught us to transform it into a source of joy, as one more way to experience intimacy with God. Isn't this the meaning of the cross and the Resurrection?

Since each one of us is unique, our relationship with God is unique as well. God uses the present moment as a way of communicating with us in an individual, particular way. God knows how to penetrate our every feeling and thought, every cell of our bodies. When we recognize God in the present moment, it becomes eternal—transcending any past or future moment to become completely intense, passionate and meaningful. The present is the meeting point between the human and the divine. It is the place where we experience the full identification of our will with God's will.

With the divine love that fills the present moment, we cannot go wrong. The present moment is where the divine is incarnated in the human, where the human is resurrected into the divine.

Fully lived, the present moment is the place that we can genuinely recognize, with the same awe as the first disciples, "It is the Lord!"

Two

JOY

Ordinary people today have material comforts and personal freedom that are greater than those of even a very rich person from any other century. We take for granted the automobile, television, radio, telephone, fax machine, dishwasher and washing machine, central heating, air conditioning and many other luxuries of modern life.

Yet this grand feast of wealth seems to do little to decrease our spiritual dissatisfaction. On the one hand, our culture feeds our "striving for more," for this is how our economy keeps humming. On the other hand, there are some things that money simply cannot buy, and these are what we most seek.

A good friend of mine described it this way: "I have every material thing I dreamed I would achieve, but what's the point when my marriage is breaking up, my health is deteriorating and my children are leaving home? The American dream was nice when it was a dream. Now it's a nightmare."

We all want happiness. We eagerly search for it, but most of the time we look in the wrong places. Happiness is big business in our culture. Entertainers, politicians, business people, even religious leaders promise us happiness, but only if we comply with their prescriptions. So we buy what they are selling, continuing our pursuit of one new pleasure or possession after another. We find ourselves caught in the "I'll be happy when..." trap: I'll be happy when I make my first million dollars, when I get my next promotion, when I get the swimming pool finished, when I own my second home, when I start my own business, when I get married, when the kids are grown, when I retire, when....

Deep joy is found in the present moment. Anxiety, worry and depression are related to the past or to the future.

We do not need to be geniuses to see that this attitude is a trap, for we feel that we are still starving, no matter how much we eat.

There is another way—much different from the "I'll be happy when..." thinking of our consumer culture—that can make us truly happy. Saint Paul put his finger on it when he told us to "Rejoice always, pray without ceasing, give thanks in all circumstances; for this is the will of God in Christ Jesus for you" (1 Thessalonians 5:16-17).

Deep joy is found in the present moment. Anxiety, worry and depression are related to the past or to the future. Living in the present moment, however, allows us to be open to all of life, including the pain, frustration and disappointment that is part of the human condition. Living now means finding God even in our apprehension and sorrow, for pain and disappointment are part of being alive.

This joy is not the kind of giddy joy we get from events or things outside ourselves. Of course, we can be happy about our successes, our health, our families. Enjoying these things are part of being in touch with God. Inner joy, however, is more than just being grateful. It radiates and transforms all that we are doing. It is joy at the deepest level, where each of us is related to the universe and to the indwelling God.

Inner joy is a state of being, of union, of ecstasy. When this joy fills our hearts, we feel united more than ever with others and we care about them all. We identify with others and become engaged with the concrete reality of their lives and the situations they encounter. We smile when another succeeds, and we weep when someone is in pain. Everything now has a dimension of depth, for we are living fully and intensely. This is the gift that Jesus brought to us.

Jesus' delight was to do the will of the Father, and every person and every event were opportunities for him to encounter his Father in the human context and return his love to his Father.

Jesus said, "I came that they might have life, and have it abundantly" (John 10:10). Jesus wants us to be fully alive, to live life "to the full," and he gave us the example of how to do this in his own life. On the eve of his crucifixion, Jesus said, "I have said these things to you that my joy may be in you, and that your joy may be complete" (John 15:11). How many times have we heard this verse, and still we picture Jesus as a sad person. Jesus said with crystal clear words that he wants his joy to be in us. He said this just a few hours before he was about to be arrested, tried, cursed, beaten, spit upon, miserably humiliated and put to death.

Jesus certainly loved life and lived it fully. But he had joy even in the midst of his suffering, for he understood that pain is part of life. What was the secret of this joyful man, who loved life so much and yet wasn't afraid of the cross? His secret was that he was wrapped at all times in his Father's loving presence. Jesus' delight was to do the will of the Father, and every person and every event were opportunities for him to encounter his Father in the human context and return his love to his Father. This is how he was able to maintain a joyful openness to the fullness of life, even in his suffering and death.

By his joy, Jesus taught us that:

1. God is unconditional love. No matter what and where we are in life and in our personal development, we are in God's image and share in divine joy. Our joy—like Jesus' joy—comes from being constantly in union with the Father.

2. God is in charge. Jesus knew that divine providence rules the world and therefore we should not worry, even if the world seems to be falling apart. This does

not mean that we should not work to make the world a better place, but it does allow us to be joyful and hopeful as we do so.

3. Love is our calling and our destiny. We must learn to love God, ourselves, and our neighbors if we are to join the dance and sing the songs of the fullness of life. "Your hearts will rejoice, and no one will take your joy from you" (John 16:22), Jesus promised.

When we "rejoice always," we can even speak about ecstasy in the mystical sense of the word. For the mystics, ecstasy (the fullness of joy) occurs when we get beyond ourselves and find ourselves immersed in God. The mystics even dare to describe their relationship with God as a profound love affair.

The presence of God in our lives cannot be taken away from us, no matter what, for we are one with God. When we recognize the divine presence in our lives, we cannot help but to "rejoice always."

Three

BLESSINGS

All of us, no matter what our current financial situation, are rich beyond belief. The treasures we possess are many and miraculous.

At what price, for example, would we value our happiness? Our life? Our most profound beliefs? Our feeling of belonging to family, community, church? The meaning we find in our lives and work? How much money would we take for our eyes, our brain, our hearing, our hands, our legs? Would we trade our loved ones for all the material possessions of the earth?

Our blessings are sometimes obvious. If we are well-fed, enjoy even a simple roof over our heads, belong to a great family, have extra money in our pockets, we recognize and appreciate—at least when we think about them—the blessings we do have. But very often these and other blessings are hardly noticed at all—unless we lose them.

Yet these blessings are as important to our spiritual lives as cornerstones are to the buildings they support.

For example, it is a blessing to have friends we can count on. They are there in good times and in bad, they understand and support us in every circumstance—even and especially when they are correcting us if we are accomplishing less than we are capable of. On the other hand, it can also be a blessing to feel alone, lonely, even abandoned, for this leads us to Jesus, who said, "I am with you always, to the end of the age" (Matthew 28:20).

All of us, no matter what our current financial situation, are rich beyond belief.

It is a blessing to experience the coming of spring, both in our environment and within us. For spring gives us the grace of hope for continuously transforming the world and being ourselves completely transformed. We can live the miracle of spring each moment of the year, if we but desire it.

It is a blessing to be able to do the right thing at the right time. How often do we feel unable to make a decision because we do not know which way is best? Then suddenly, we are inspired to move this way or that, as if we were touched by an angel.

It is sometimes a blessing to fail to get what we want. These are the occasions when we thank God that our initial prayer was not answered according to our will or desire, because what happened instead was so much better than what we were asking for.

It can be a blessing to feel pain and soreness. A body that does not give signals of malaise can be downright dangerous to our very existence. Likewise, it can be a blessing to know sorrow and grief. Although painful, deep sadness visits only those who have loved deeply. No one likes to grieve, but to grieve is to experience caring, sharing and being vulnerable to their divine depths.

It is a blessing to be able to relate to children in many special ways and to play even a small role in their lives. It is a blessing to give them something of ourselves without expecting—or even wanting—anything back in return. It is a blessing to trust young people and to let them learn from their own experiences as well as from ours. It is a blessing to offer them help when they need it and to let our strengths supplement theirs.

It is a blessing to know when to speak up and when to be silent, when to intervene and when to stay away. It is a blessing to be ourselves and to let others be themselves. But it is also a blessing to try to make the world a better place.

❈❈ ❈❈ ❈❈ ❈❈

If we can open our minds and hearts and join the chorus of the universe in a prayerful song of thanksgiving for the many blessings God is bestowing upon us at all times, we may be surprised to realize how rich we really are.

❈❈ ❈❈ ❈❈ ❈❈

It is a blessing to hear the steps of the newspaper delivery person bringing his or her daily gift to our doors. It is a blessing to read a warm letter or a quick e-mail from a faraway relative or friend, or to receive a telephone call from someone who truly cares about us.

It is a blessing to have useful work to do, the right tools and equipment to do it with, and the energy and talent to make it productive.

It is a blessing to wash dishes and observe rainbows in the soap bubbles, to smell fresh-cut flowers on a dining room table, to observe a star from a bedroom window, to hear the sounds of silence on a tranquil night.

It is a blessing to have a past, a present and a future.

It is a blessing to live thankfully. Indeed, all our prayer should be thanksgiving-in-action: open, loving and full of joy. "Give thanks in all circumstances," recommended Saint Paul, "for this is the will of God in Christ Jesus for you" (1 Thessalonians 5:18). If we can open our minds and hearts and join the chorus of the universe in a prayerful song of thanksgiving for the many blessings God is bestowing upon us at all times, we may be surprised to realize how rich we really are.

Four

SIMPLICITY

Living simply is the easiest, most direct way to attain freedom and joy. When we succeed at living simply, we realize that we do not really need most of the innumerable things we usually consider necessities. In fact, we realize these necessities became so only after we acquired them, sometimes at a very high cost to our souls.

Our society is crazy about the grandiose, the glamorous, the competitive, the marketable, the visibly successful. These multiple pressures all work in our culture to make our lives very complex, while living simply helps us become aware (or aware again) of what really matters to us.

Here is a list of some of the things that can contribute to complicating our lives:

- credit cards
- big houses and mortgages

- latest fashions and products
- expensive clothes and fancy cars
- high-tech radios, televisions and video systems
- the Internet and computers
- telephones and wireless phones
- fax and answering machines, call waiting
- sixty-hour work weeks
- lack of time to spend with family and friends
- jobs we don't particularly enjoy
- junk mail, e-mail, telephone solicitors
- busyness, anger, worries, fears

*Our society is crazy
about the grandiose, the
glamorous, the competitive,
the marketable, the
visibly successful.*

We can all add hundreds, even thousands, of things to this list that make our lives hectic and unfocused and therefore restricted and unhappy. We find ourselves exhausted from obtaining and maintaining them. Yet even when we start to "clean our closets" to get rid of some of these distractions, we often fill the new space with other things. We want to trim our commitments, but instead we fill the void with other tasks and possessions. At the end of the day, however, we still feel that we didn't make enough money, didn't run hard enough, are somehow missing the train of life.

There is another way to live. It is called "living simply." When we live simply, there is a shift in focus. Our concern becomes faithfulness rather than success—faithfulness to our true selves and to what God calls us to be. Letting God become involved in our lives on this level—totally and without restrictions—allows us to concentrate on "only one thing" (Luke 10:42), as Jesus challenged Martha.

Jesus taught that total dependence on God will provide us with our real wealth. "Look at the birds of the air; they neither sow nor reap nor gather into barns, and yet your heavenly Father feeds them. And can any of you by worrying add a single hour to your span of life? And why do you worry about clothing? Consider the lilies of the field, how they grow; they neither toil nor spin, yet I tell you, even Solomon in all his glory was not clothed like one of these. But if God so clothes the grass of the field, which is alive today and tomorrow is thrown into the oven, will he not much more clothe you—you of little faith?" (Matthew 6:26-30).

Becoming aware of the presence of God in our lives may seem a difficult thing amidst all our serious worries, important tasks and driving ambitions. Here are two tips that may help to simplify our lives:

1. Prioritize. Sooner or later, we have to ask ourselves what the point is of all our busyness. What is really important? What ultimately matters to us? Then we have to let go, little by little, of all the things that aren't critical to our spiritual development. We know from experience how difficult it is to get rid of things we've worked hard to accumulate, but if they are in the way of who we want to be then we need to dedicate our best efforts to those things that really matter. We may find that our deepest joy may come not from adding things but in subtracting them.

2. Reflect. Even if we cannot go on a formal retreat or spend a lot of time in formal meditation, most of us can find fifteen minutes a day to reflect on what we are doing. We need to take that time to slow down, to do nothing, to be unproductive if you will. For only when we do this can we recall what our real goals are in life. Somehow, when we get back in touch with the driving force in our lives, many of the other things that we thought were important and necessary start to drop away one by one. When we

know what our life's work is all about, we start to simplify naturally, earnestly and effectively.

To live simply is not necessarily to escape to the woods and live a primitive lifestyle. What is the point of the most remote hermitage if we take with us our worries, our fears, our greed, our confusion? We would then still be not at all free. Our joy would be false.

Jesus taught that total dependence on God will provide us with our real wealth.

What we need to do is decide what is enough and then stick to it in our daily lives. This will bring us great freedom and true joy.

Five

WONDER

By awakening our sense of wonder, we can catch God at work in the here and now. Wonder is a way of perceiving that makes our spirits, minds and hearts marvel at a world we thought we understood.

We wonder when we witness nature's immense beauty and bounty or watch a baby bird fly for the first time or are enchanted by a full moon sparkling over a quiet lake on a serene summer night.

We wonder when we think over our old patterns of living and give them new meanings, suggesting to ourselves that maybe there's more to what we are doing every day than just biding time or running in place.

We wonder at the paradoxes of life: how by giving we receive, by suffering we heal, by weeping we find joy, by losing we win. "For those who want to save their life will lose it, and those who lose their life for my sake will find it" (Matthew 16:25), as Jesus said.

We wonder when we find hope anew, after all our hope has gone. We wonder when laughter replaces sadness and despair: "When the Lord restored the fortunes of Zion, we were like those who dream. Then our mouth was filled with laughter, and our tongue with shouts of joy" (Psalm 126:1-2).

※ ※ ※ ※

Wonder is a way of perceiving that makes our spirits, minds and hearts marvel at a world we thought we understood.

※ ※ ※ ※

We wonder when we see, hear, taste, smell, touch and witness the miracle of the present moment, when we are satisfied by the occurrence of what we had been waiting for or surprised by something we had never anticipated, when we transform ourselves by expanding our vision beyond our wildest imagination.

We wonder at the transformation of simple colors into a piece of art, the arrangement of unrelated notes into an inspiring symphony, the capture of our hearts by the singing of a human voice, a book that contains ideas never before thought—at least by us.

We wonder at the little things we do for one another that make each of us happy.

We wonder when we are born and when we die.

We wonder when we wonder.

Our sense of wonder can be continuously nurtured and expanded if we get in touch with God's creation. Here are some simple suggestions:

1. Appreciate small pleasures. Open an observing eye and see the tree in front of your door, the blue sky, the green grass. Enjoy them all. Listen to the song of a bird. Smell the fragrance of a field. Taste freshly baked bread. Stroke the silky hair of a cat or dog. Listen to the sounds of the day awakening.

2. Learn the trick of "I-was-blind-but-now-I-see"—observing without prejudgment nor preestablished conceptions nor negative emotions the world around you, as if for the first time. "One thing I do know, that though I was blind, now I see" (John 9: 25), said the man born blind.

3. Do what you love. The things you *need* to do are necessary in order to live. But the things you *love* to do give you the very *reason* for living. By doing what you love, you increase your health and energy level and therefore your imagination and creativity.

4. Care for yourself. Be gentle with yourself. Say loving words to yourself, such as, "I accept you," "I love you," and "Tomorrow you are going to be even better." Instead of being your own worst enemy, be your own best friend.

5. Forgive yourself. When you make a mistake, fall or relapse, treat yourself with great patience and love. This is how to accelerate the healing process.

6. Express yourself. Let the child within you express his or her feelings in the form of drawing, playing music, singing, writing or acting. Let others know how you feel about them in a childlike way.

7. Play. Play somehow unites us all. Adults and children, men and women, humans and animals all deepen our connectedness when we play together.

With a sense of wonder we expand our thinking, deepen our insight, and embark on the long journey of searching for the source of all sources, the cause of all causes. When we develop a sense of wonder, we intensify our search for meaning and purpose and discover dimensions of ourselves of which we were not aware. We realize that there is more to life than what appears on the surface, and we begin to see the world as a dynamic energy—ever evolving, ever blooming.

With a sense of wonder we expand our thinking, deepen our insight, and embark on the long journey of searching for the source of all sources, the cause of all causes.

Wonder sees in other human beings the same needs as our own—the needs for love, forgiveness, reverence, justice and peace. Wonder notices our sameness and uncovers ways to improve our common condition. Wonder finds in every problem an opportunity for healing other hearts with the touch of divinity.

Wonder draws out the holy within ourselves and others. It seeks the worthier, the healthier, the newer, the better.

Wonder proclaims the Incarnate God in the human condition, the Holy Spirit at work in the transformation of the world. It allows a compelling sense of reverence, awe and gratitude to invade us, and we become eyewitnesses of the divine presence in the here and now.

Wonder engenders prayerful lives. It finds epiphanies in everything.

When the presence of God becomes so overwhelming, we cannot help but kneel. An unsophisticated and guileless "Wow!' is the prayer of wonder.

Six

IMPERFECTION

Saints—like the rest of us—are imperfect, unfinished human beings. What makes them different is that they are on fire with love, for God and for others.

Saints do not have a "prayer" life and a "regular" life. They live one united life. Their prayer life is their ordinary life, and their ordinary life is their prayer life. Their contemplation is their action, and their action is their contemplation.

Saints are people who use all of their human potential, but they let their divine potential do most of the work. They strive for perfection, but they know how imperfect they are. Their ideal is not to be without weakness or fault, but to be holy despite their failings. Their "perfection" is not realized by escaping their humanness but by becoming fully human, just as their master, Jesus, was fully human. "Learn from me; for I am gentle and humble in heart" (Matthew 11:29), he said, and saints are the ones who do.

What does human perfection mean anyway? It is not mere conformism to a set of precepts, counsels, ascetic practices, moral principles, legal rules or accurately performed rituals. All these have meaning only when they are related to the overriding Christian commandment of love. Love is the "big deal" in the kingdom of God.

Perfection is not achieved by attempting to deny a self that is undesirable or a human condition that is unavoidable. No one becomes a saint by denying his or her own realities. Nor does perfection mean saying or doing the right things at the right times. One does not become a saint by turning into an efficient religious machine. Certainly, traditional religious observances deserve admiration and encouragement, but they are only a framework for the spiritual life. We can have the best hearth in the world, but what good is it if there is no fire in it? It is only when the Holy Spirit gains possession of a heart that a person become a saint.

The most amazing thing, however, is that we Christians are called—by virtue of our baptism—to become saints. Don't scoff. The Second Vatican Council said, "Fortified by so many and such powerful means of salvation, all the faithful, whatever their condition or state, are called by the Lord, each in his or her own way, to that perfect holiness whereby the Father Himself is perfect" *(Dogmatic Constitution on the Church, 11).*

Holiness—and therefore sainthood—is not the monopoly of popes, bishops, priests, monks, men and women religious. Nor is it reserved for martyrs, founders of religious orders, and Catholic monarchs. It is not only for the rich, or even the famous. There can be, as in the title of Benedictine Father Albert Holtz's book, *A Saint on Every Corner.*

※ ※ ※ ※

Perfection is not achieved by attempting to deny a self that is undesirable or a human condition that is unavoidable.

※ ※ ※ ※

Not that we will necessarily know who they are. Sanctity, like prayer, is best practiced behind closed doors. Still, all of us, no matter what our state in life, are called to become saints by living fully the particular life in which we find ourselves. Holiness can be practiced in the most unlikely of places—kitchens, offices, streetcorners—and by all sorts of people—parents, spouses, children, teachers, farmers, secretaries.

Even our very real human imperfection is not an insurmountable obstacle to holiness. Saints, by definition, are imperfect, since saints, by definition, are human beings. For humans, there is always a gap between the ideal and the real, the not-yet and the already here. Saints are merely those humans who, with God's help, try to close this gap.

For humans, there is always a gap between the ideal and the real, the not-yet and the already here. Saints are merely those humans who, with God's help, try to close this gap.

We do not need to be perfect to be saints. What is required (not that this is easy) is to cultivate the awareness of the divine presence in every place, at any time. Saints are those who stop living two lives—one "spiritual" and the other "ordinary." For saints, all life is "charged with the grandeur of God," as poet Gerard Manley Hopkins wrote.

For them, grace is everywhere and everything is gift. That is how they can "pray without ceasing" (1 Thessalonians 5:17), as Saint Paul suggested. Their lives *are* their prayer.

Saints are earthy-mystics, incarnational-transcendentalists, contemplatives-in-action. In a way, whoever is alive to God's love is already a saint, whether he or she lives in castle or cave, works as bank president or teller, sits in a university's tenured chair or a taxi's well-worn driver's seat.

It is foolish to try to describe a clear formula for holiness, but the one thing that surely makes the difference between saints and non-saints is that saints are the ones who have jumped into the ocean of God's love and come out transfigured. Then, almost without thinking or even trying, they begin to pull the rest of us out of our loneliness and fear by infecting us with the love they've already experienced.

Saints are human, sure. And they are imperfect, just like the rest of us. But they are all bold lovers.

Seven

LONELINESS

Why are so many of us unhappy in spite of having so much? Why is the "Don Quixote" in us never satisfied, always looking for another windmill to conquer? Why do we feel so jealous, so possessive, so compulsive? Loneliness could be the answer.

Our culture offers unprecedented means of communication—television, radio, telephone, the Internet. But at the same time almost everything we do promotes our being alone. We prefer self-service at the gas station, fast food at the drive-through, and mail-ordering from home. Sometimes we'd rather leave a message on an answering machine than talk to a live person. Let's face it, the solitary is flourishing in the high-tech global village.

Loneliness has nothing to do with solitude, however. We can feel lonely when alone, but we can also feel lonely in the midst of a crowd.

I read a story once about a mystic who lived alone on a far mountain for a great many years. One day a reporter went to see him and asked, "Aren't you terribly lonely out here by yourself?" The holy man's immediate reply was, "I wasn't lonely until you came!" This answer may seem rude, but it makes the point: Loneliness has nothing to do with merely being alone. Its secret lies elsewhere.

❦— ✦— ✦— ✦

Loneliness is a psychological and spiritual alarm bell that tells us that something is going wrong in our lives.

❦— ✦— ✦— ✦

Saint Augustine described the human condition this way: "Thou hast made us for Thyself, and our hearts are restless until they rest in Thee." So perhaps the profound loneliness many people feel is really a deep longing for God. The mystic in the story, even though he was alone, was not lonely. He was one with his God.

Loneliness is related to the lack of love in our lives. We are lonely whenever and wherever we fear loving. This can manifest itself in different forms of behavior—avoidance, running away, complaining, jealousy, dissatisfaction, narcissism, snobbery, competitiveness, lying, stealing, controlling, judging, violence and so forth.

Loneliness has a way of affecting our entire being: our hopes, ambitions, dreams, vitality, wants, lifestyles, ways of eating and sleeping. Stoop-shouldered, sad-eyed, lonely people seem to be frozen at their center. They are afraid to love, although they want love so badly.

There are some ways we can go about alleviating loneliness. Here are a few:

1. Build bridges, not walls. Do not say such things as "No one loves me" or "I am unlovable" or "Who is ever going to love me?" Such words are prescriptions for loneliness. In saying them, we create walls between ourselves and others. Instead, say positive things about yourself like "I am loved" or "Many people love me." In this way, you will build bridges, not walls.

2. Remember that loneliness cannot be overcome by "getting" more things. Adding new possessions to your life—even more friends—will not change your outlook. Only inner work will do that. Loneliness is not overcome by external additions but by internal concentration on what is really important in life. Make God the foundation of your life.

3. Live in oneness. When we recognize the spiritual unity of all persons, all things, all life, then loneliness loses its reason to exist. It is a great illusion that we each have a separate existence, fate and destiny. The truth is that all of us are integrated into a whole with everyone else. We must learn to live in that oneness if we are to overcome loneliness.

4. Cultivate solitude. We often think that busyness is the normal human way, that life is supposed to be a continuous do, do, do. Even vacations sometimes become a form of work. But if you are to overcome loneliness, you must learn to embrace silence. Solitude gives us the opportunity to come face to face with ourselves and with God. When we discover that we love ourselves and that God loves us, we can be lonely no more.

5. Let your love be the driving force in your life. As the author of the First Letter of John said, "Love has no room for fear" (1 John 4:18). Love is the most fantastic energy known to humankind. It is the definition of God! And since we are created in God's image, we are supposed to be love, too.

When we relate to everything through God, we become whole and holy. God is Trinity, community, social life. God is relational. God is never lonely. We are not supposed to be lonely either: "Our hearts are restless until they rest in Thee."

So perhaps the profound loneliness many people feel is really a deep longing for God.

Loneliness is a psychological and spiritual alarm bell that tells us that something is going wrong in our lives. We need to take action before we are consumed by the chronic disability that is loneliness.

Eight

FRIENDSHIP

It seems crucial that each of us have at least one essential friend. No life can be complete without experiencing the joy of true friendship. We usually take friends for granted, but in fact they are graces that require steadfast and striving participation on our part.

Friends are of critical importance for our healthy living at the physical level as well as the psychological, emotional and spiritual levels. Friends help us live healthier, happier and longer. "Your friend," wrote Kahlil Gibran, "is your needs answered."

There is now strong scientific evidence that close ties to friends helps prevent illnesses and actually can increase the chances of surviving a malignant disease. Certainly, by reducing the effects of stress, friends play a major role in the full recovery process of each individual. The reverse can also be true. Isolated people are much more at risk for sickness and mortality.

Professor Eugene Kennedy, the brilliant psychologist and best-selling author, says, "Friendship has a profound effect on your physical well-being. Having good relationships improves health and lifts depressions. You don't necessarily need drugs or medical treatment to accomplish this—just friends."

The gift of friendship benefits every one of us, no matter what our personal situation is. Friendship fulfills our need to connect with others at many meaningful levels. It rescues us from loneliness by providing the joy of shared experiences and the support on which we can lean when we desperately need it. Friends are there in health and in sickness, in good times and in bad times, on wealthy days and on poor nights. A good friend listens, understands, cares and shares with a loving heart and an open mind. With a good friend our joy doubles, our sadness shrinks, our dreams set wings and our worries surrender their fears.

Only with a true friend can we learn the pleasure of selfless receiving. For once we have experienced the pleasure of giving for its own sake—without any obligation or expectation of return—we are in a position to accept similar largess from a friend, for we want to provide him or her with the same pleasure. When we receive with gratitude, our friend's heart expands with great joy. Friendship is a two-way exchange, a continuously shifting process from giving to receiving and back again.

Friendship's love has a special flavor other loves—like that of parents for children or brother for sister—do not have. Friends allow us to discover that we are lovable and that life is rich. We also learn that friends are lovable, too, and that the rich diversity of human life is more fulfilling when understood and shared.

With a good friend our joy doubles, our sadness shrinks, our dreams set wings and our worries surrender their fears.

Friendship was very important to Jesus. He pushed it to the extreme—to the point that he would even die for it: "This is my commandment, that you love one another as I have loved you. No one has greater love than this, to lay down one's life for one's friends. You are my friends if you do what I command you. I do not call you servants any longer, because the servant does not know what the master is doing; but I have called you friends, because I have made known to you everything that I have heard from my Father" (John 15:12-15).

Jesus is still available to be our friend. We can confide in him in times of sorrow and sadness and rejoice with him in times of joy and celebration. In *The Imitation of Christ,* the fifteenth-century mystic Thomas à Kempis expressed his friendship with Jesus thus: "Love Him, and keep Him for thy friend, who, when all go away, will not forsake thee, nor suffer thee to perish in the end....Keep close to Jesus both in life and in death, and commit thyself unto His faithfulness, who, when all fail, can alone help thee....Without a friend thou canst not live well; and if Jesus be not above all a friend to thee, thou shalt be indeed sad and desolate."

In Christian life, friendship is not only a source of great joy and fulfillment, it is also a path to unification, communion and peace among all people. Friendship is the expression of God's reign in the most human of terms and in the most realistic way possible. Friendship belongs to the entire human family, as it transcends all barriers and frontiers: "There is no longer Jew or Greek, there is no longer slave or free, there is no longer male and female; for all of you are one in Christ Jesus" (Galatians 3:28). Friends who have real love for one another participate in divine life; their friendship is a sacrament, a sign of God's presence among us.

Friendship is not easy to achieve. It requires effort, thought, openness, vulnerability, and even the willingness to risk love. Friendships do not spring up like flowers and grass. They have to be cultivated very carefully and need time to bloom and grow and bear fruit. Neither are friends manufactured. Genuine caring, sustained attention to one another's needs, loyal mutual commitment, willingness to listen and spend time, little gestures of kindness and goodness, openness and acceptance—these provide the space in the heart where friends find a home.

In Christian life, friendship is not only a source of great joy and fulfillment, it is also a path to unification, communion and peace among all people.

We are all fellow travelers on the long journey of life. Friends help one another, share with one another, encourage one another, support one another and love one another. Friends bring joy and implant hope. Friends are what make God's reign come more quickly. Friends are grace, gift, blessing, sacrament. They are life's best medicine.

Nine

Money

Certainly, we need money. We need it to provide for our needs and the needs of others. We need it in order to accomplish many good things. But as Saint Paul warned us, "the love of money is the root of all kinds of evil, and in their eagerness to be rich some have wandered away from the faith and pierced themselves with many pains" (1 Timothy 6:10). Money can be God's abundant bounty or the hidden corrupter of our souls.

What is money? Nothing, really. Everything, maybe. In itself, money is nothing—a worthless piece of paper, a bit of common metal. When it represents something else, however, it can be a measure of the meaning and value we assign to various things.

In "the good old days," people used to exchange sheep for wheat, eggs for fruit, labor for a meal and a place to sleep. This is exactly what we still do today, but money makes the exchange much easier. So money is nothing but the symbol of the exchange between a seller and a buyer, done on a much more complex, global economic stage.

❦ ⊱⋇⊰ ⊱⋇⊰ ⊱⋇❧

No matter what we do for a living, our real business is to release our splendor— which is God living in us.

❦ ⊱⋇⊰ ⊱⋇⊰ ⊱⋇❧

Money means nothing if it doesn't circulate. The miser, sitting in his shack counting his gold in absolute misery, is a horrible waste of spiritual potential. When money is exchanged—when it passes from hand to hand, from business to business, from country to country—energy flows with it. It is this energy of exchange that allows us to approach money as a source of spiritual life.

Greed and selfishness are what make money a symbol of deterioration and destruction; love and detachment make it a way toward interconnectedness and progress. If we allow money to provide us with confidence, security, freedom from want, and generosity, its possession and use can be an authentic spiritual experience. Money can be a pathway of our spiritual development.

Here are some thoughts on the "holy" use of money:

1. Money is vision. Try to have the mentality and attitude of the wealthy person—not in spending money foolishly but in knowing that you can afford all that you really need. See your life as bountiful and abundant, rather than poor and limited. We are rich when—and only when—we are in a state of wholeness and oneness with the source of all things.

2. Money is movement. The more you give, the more you will receive. The more you receive, the more you can give. Only in circulation is money holy. Put your money on the move. Stretch it—and yourself—as much as you can. Set clear long and short term financial goals, then go for them. It is monetary movement that leads to spiritual growth.

3. Money is preparation. Money has its own rules, methods, and regulations. Go to school, ask the experts, read about money-making. Learn about budgets, savings, record-keeping, investing. Keep your eyes and ears open, use all your good ideas, skills, time and energy. Keep track of every single transaction you make, because God is in all of them.

4. Money is abundance. Having more money for yourself does not necessarily mean you are taking it from someone else. There is no limit to the number of

times money can turn over, the energy it can generate, the good that it can produce. "I came that they may have life, and have it abundantly" (John 10:10), Jesus promised.

5. Money is gratefulness. Focus on your many blessings, rather than on what you lack. God's grace will continue to shower upon you when you are grateful for what you already have. Give thanks for your "daily bread"—which has been given to you as pure gift.

6. Money is surrender. Link yourself to the source of all things, that from which all energy is generated. Align your projects with the flow of the universe's energy. Pray "Thy will be done" each day, recognizing that how you use your money can be a sign of the unfolding of the divine will.

7. Money is simple. For you to have more money, one of two things have to happen: you have to find ways to increase your income, or—better yet—you have to find ways to reduce your expenses. You do not really need a great deal of possessions to live a good life. Put your fiscal energy in the direction of those things that really matter, and you will find yourself eliminating unnecessary and irrelevant expenses. Presto! You'll have more money.

8. Money is myth. Money does not equal happiness, love, power, freedom, security or self-worth. Money can certainly help in achieving these goals, but it is a myth that money in and of itself can deliver any of these things. If you can remember this, you will save yourself a lot of headaches, guilt and fear. You will use money in ways that reflect your deepest convictions and values.

Greed and selfishness are what make money a symbol of deterioration and destruction; love and detachment make it a way toward interconnectedness and progress.

Like all of us, Jesus and his disciples had their expenses. Often they were supported by others, including Mary of Magdala, Joanna, Susanna, and "many others, who provide for them out of their resources" (Luke 8:3). These women apparently knew how to use their wealth to help spread the Good News. So Jesus was not against money itself. He was against placing money ahead of God: "Strive first for the kingdom of God and his righteousness, and all these things will be given to you as well" (Matthew 6:33).

God cannot fail us. No matter what we do for a living, our real business is to release our splendor—which is God living in us. Money can be an external expression of the flow of divine energy. That energy is the *arcanum,* the philosopher's magic stone that can either turn everything to gold or reduce everything to ashes.

Ten

IDENTITY

Most of our individual identities are inherited or borrowed. In many ways, we are like garments others have used before. Our individual thoughts, principles and lifestyle are not really ours. We assimilated them from parents, teachers, friends and the surrounding culture. Unconscious forces condition us to appear and behave in ways not our own.

Without stretching this simple truth too far, we are—more or less—living others' lives. In a way, we are becoming copies of them. In so doing, however, we prevent ourselves from becoming our real selves.

Discovering the true self may be the most difficult task in life. Jesus certainly called us to live a life of honesty and integrity. He told us to say "yes" when we mean "yes" and "no" when we mean "no." He wanted us to conduct our lives in accordance with his spiritual vision of justice, concern for others, and love. He recommended that our actions not be for personal gain and advised us to abstain from compromising our spiritual principles to our political or financial self-interests.

≈⊱ ⊰≈⊱ ⊰≈⊱ ⊰≈

*Discovering the true self
may be the most
difficult task in life.*

≈⊱ ⊰≈⊱ ⊰≈⊱ ⊰≈

In order to do that, we have to know who we really are at the deepest core of our being. Here are a few suggestions that might enhance your search for self:

1. Be yourself, as often as you can. Stop the business of playing games with yourself and others. Be honest, genuine and straightforward. Feel, think and act according to the values and beliefs you stand for. You will be amazed at the person you discover.

2. Be vulnerable. Opening the door for others to know the real you allows them to be vulnerable with you in return. It is not necessary to be this way with every person you meet, but sharing yourself deeply— over a long period of time—with your spouse, a

parent, a sibling or a good friend is absolutely necessary for your own self-knowledge.

3. Love yourself. To pretend to love others and even life itself is hypocritical and an illusion if you don't also have true love for yourself. The ability to love others is conditioned by the ability to love yourself. Remember that no matter whom you are with, what you are doing or where you are going, the only constant that remains is yourself. You might as well be good company!

4. Judge yourself by who you are, not by what you do. You are not your achievements, nor your bank account. You needn't depend on your position or possessions to measure your success. Think about your intrinsic worth—without "gilding the lily," so to speak.

5. Do what the real you is meant to do. Let your actions match your good thoughts, words, and intentions. This will reveal who you really are—to both yourself and others. Banish hypocrisy, celebrate integrity.

Even Jesus was interested in finding out who people thought he was: "And you, who do you say that I am?"

(Matthew 16:15). So it would seem logical that he would want us to know who we are, too. Jesus calls us to our deepest identity, which is to be sons and daughters of the Most High.

If we are aware of this identity, we recognize that we are created in the very image and likeness of God. When we see ourselves as God sees us, all our other images of ourselves fade into insignificance. We extricate ourselves from all outside influences. We become completely free to pursue who we really are.

Jesus calls us to our deepest identity, which is to be sons and daughters of the Most High.

People who know their identity are rebellious. They unmask all that is false. They refuse to be conditioned. They reject robot lives. Their prayer is a declaration that there will be no interference with the divine action that occurs in and through them.

Eleven

SLEEP

How we sleep reveals much of who we are and what is happening in our spiritual life. Our sleep is a mirror of our physical, mental, emotional and spiritual state of being.

"Early to bed and early to rise," Ben Franklin once advised, but is this still possible when life after dark has become more and more attractive? Electric lights, television, automobiles, theaters, and other distractions all serve to keep us awake, to "lighten" the dark of our nights to the point that we all get less and less sleep.

The overstimulation and excesses of modern living— the noise and lights, the caffeine and alcohol—are not, however, the main reasons our rest is being disturbed. The essential factor is ourselves. Indeed, it is we who choose our lifestyle, who want to stay up all night, who cannot sleep because we are worried, preoccupied, obsessed or nervous. We are the ones who allow the continuous tension of trying to meet appointments, deadlines and expectations, of trying to present a good image and convince others of our qualifications, to result in lack of sleep. We are afraid to take even a minute of respite during the day—much less a nap—because we believe that every unproductive minute is a wasted one.

The monks and mystics of old used to deny themselves sleep as an ascetic practice, but it may be just as profitable a spiritual path to make sure that we are well-rested, for only then can we be attuned to the divine life that is always present in the moment.

It is almost as if we think the planet will fall apart if we do not continuously watch over it. We do a hundred different things with our waking time, yet we fail to focus on the essential and real purpose of life.

No wonder, then, that we do not sleep well. Conse-
quently, it's also no wonder that we feel irritable and lack
the vital mental sharpness and zest for living we used to
have. We feel sick and tired of doing the same things
again and again. We suffer the unpleasant feeling of having been "drained." We feel exhausted, depressed, hope-
less. Our mental functions deteriorate, our ethical stan-
dards sink. Much or all of this is from lack of sleep!

Sufficient sleep, on the other hand, protects our health.
Some studies have suggested that there is a biochemical
link between deep sleep and the immune system. Somehow, good sleepers appear to be more resistant to viral
and bacterial infections and possibly even to cancer. It is
certain that sleep is needed for normal tissue repair and
revitalization. Sleep also helps the brain to refocus. When
we are sleep-deprived, our thoughts become disorganized,
memory lapses, judgment suffers, and irritability and confusion reign. Sleep helps us restore ourselves when we
feel physically, mentally or even spiritually exhausted.

Yes, sleep can be a spiritual pathway. The monks and
mystics of old used to deny themselves sleep as an ascetic
practice, but it may be just as profitable a spiritual path to
make sure that we are well-rested, for only then can we
be attuned to the divine life that is always present in the
moment. A good night's rest helps us get where we are
going at a better pace and in a more secure way. We

manage our time, our thoughts and our goals better if we sleep well the night before. We work more efficiently and create things of better quality. We are more in control and more easily inspired—all elements of a healthy and holy spiritual life.

※━ ━━ ━━ ━❖

> *We need to let God be in charge of the universe, and sleep is a prayer that acknowledges just that.*

※━ ━━ ━━ ━❖

How much sleep do we need? That depends on our age, state of health, physique, personality, and the kind of work we do. In general, most people in normal physical condition need seven to eight hours a night in order to function at their best. There are many recommendations for improving our sleep. Indeed, it is usually not enough to just lay down in a bed and close our eyes. For better quality sleep we need to have a consistent routine: go to bed by a certain hour, make sure the temperature of the room is right for us, shut off all the lights, shut out as much noise as possible, have the right pillow and mattress, stick to a light dinner beforehand.

This is the hard part, however. If we want to sleep peacefully, we need to be able to leave our worries outside the door of our house or at least outside our bedroom, and this is where God can help.

The Bible has perhaps the best prescription for good rest and peace of mind:

> Unless the LORD builds the house,
>> those who build it labour in vain....
> It is in vain that you rise up early
>> and go late to rest,
> eating the bread of anxious toil;
>> for he gives sleep to his beloved.
>
> Psalm 127:1-2

Jesus himself took a nap while his companions were struggling in fear in the storm at sea (see Mark 4:35-41). Was Jesus indifferent, careless, reckless? No, he was just without anxiety. He was worry free, and when we are worry free we, too, can sleep through anything. Jesus knew that his Father was in control, and that was fine with him. In a sense, sleep for Jesus was just another way of praying, another way of trusting and counting on God.

So, a short rest, a little nap, a good night's sleep are not things that should make us feel guilty or even spiritually incomplete. We need to let God be in charge of the universe, and sleep is a prayer that acknowledges just that. To sleep soundly proves that we are giving God—not ourselves—time to save the world.

If we trust and love God through our sleep, our life will smooth out and our ordinary troubles will fade away. We will be focused on the real purpose of our life. As it says in the Book of Proverbs:

> Then you will walk on your way securely
> and your foot will not stumble.
> If you sit down, you will not be afraid:
> when you lie down, your sleep will be sweet.
>
> Proverbs 3:23-24

Sleeping constitutes one-third of our life. What a wasted time if we fail to make it a prayer. We sleep because we are tired, but we also sleep because we can trust God. When we turn control over to God, our "sleep will be sweet" indeed.

Twelve

Senses

Each of our five senses can be a pathway to God. When we sharpen our senses spiritually, we can experience God in a real, physical way.

Sharpening our senses does not depend solely on our own efforts, of course. The primary stimulus of the transformation of our senses into instruments of spiritual perception is the Incarnation of Jesus Christ. Because the divine became flesh, our senses can be vehicles for encountering the divine in our daily life. Isn't this an essential part of what the sacraments are all about?

After the Incarnation, spirituality is no longer the opposite of materiality. It is not even separate from it. In the Incarnation, spirit and body became one in a very unique way, and therefore Christian spiritual life must now include the use of our senses—but in new ways. Thomas Merton said it best in *No Man Is an Island:* "The first step in the interior life, nowadays, is not, as some might imagine, learning *not* to see and taste and hear and feel things. On the contrary, what we must do is begin by unlearning our wrong ways of seeing, tasting, feeling, and so forth, and acquire a few of the right ones."

※━ ━━ ━━ ━━

The primary stimulus of the transformation of our senses into instruments of spiritual perception is the Incarnation of Jesus Christ.

※━ ━━ ━━ ━━

For example, it takes a special kind of effort to be able to "see" the divine activity in our lives. As the writer of the Letter to the Hebrews put it, "By faith we understand that the worlds were prepared by the word of God, so that what is seen was made from things that are not visible" (Hebrews 11:3). The task of spirituality is to open our eyes and see the way Jesus sees, as he did with the widow at Nain: "When the Lord saw her, he had compassion for her and said to her, 'Do not weep'" (Luke 7:13).

In every situation, we must stop, think, and ask ourselves: Do I see in this situation the hand of God? What is

God's purpose in this? How can I participate in the fulfillment of that purpose? When we are able to see in this way, the invisible presence of God is manifest. To see with the eyes of Christ is to live the essence of Christian ministry, and in so doing we make the divine presence visible to others in the midst of all their fears, worries, concerns, sufferings, joys and hopes.

Likewise, we must train ourselves to hear in a new way. God talked with Abraham through angelic visitors (see Genesis 18). Moses heard God in a burning bush (see Exodus 3). Elijah recognized God in "a sound of sheer silence" (1 Kings 19:12). Jesus heard a voice from the heavens (see Mark 1:11). God talks to us, too, but we must attune our senses to hear it. Only then can we say, "Speak, for your servant is listening" (1 Samuel 3:10).

We can improve our sense of hearing by first silencing the other noises in our lives. We need to go to a tranquil lake some quiet evening, when a clear sky is filled with sparkling stars and nothing is disturbing our attention. Then we must listen to the water, the sky, the air, straining to hear and understand. Only then will we experience the sound of the universe.

We can also hear God in our own breath. To inhale and exhale is not a choice. If we stop, we die. The first time we inhale is at birth, and the last time we exhale is at death. Our very existence is tied to our breathing, which is why the masters of meditation consider the breathing process to be the first step in awareness, mindfulness, and integration of mind, body and spirit.

Even our sense of smell can help define our spirituality. Each of us smells things differently—according to hereditary factors, moods, medications, health situations and special diets. We each use perfume, incense, flowers, even fruits to add to the atmosphere of our environment. Saint Paul said that there is a "fragrance that comes from knowing [Christ]. For we are the aroma of Christ to God among those who are being saved and among those who are perishing" (2 Corinthians 2:14-15).

Spiritual life is merely ordinary life lived with God at its center.

When we sharpen our sense of smell, we can receive more easily the breath of life that is the gift of the Holy Spirit. God can be as close to us as our own breathing. We can actually "smell" the divine presence if we sniff right!

In a similar way, we can also "taste" God: "O taste and see that the LORD is good" (Psalm 34:8). In a society in which a great number of us have eating or drinking disorders, we may have lost our sensitivity to spiritual tasting. But we can get it back.

To really delight in our sense of taste, however, a few requirements must be included on the menu. First of all, we are supposed to be hungry: "Blessed are those who hunger and thirst for righteousness, for they will be filled" (Matthew 5:6). Next, we must be ready for change. When we taste of a truly spiritual banquet, we cannot then go back to bland spiritual food. We become different people, and we extend our new selves to others.

Jesus enjoyed eating and drinking, but in the Eucharist he opened up the deepest meaning of sharing a meal: When we experience real fellowship, a sense of belonging, and a familial and communal connectedness, then we know what incarnational spirituality is all about.

Finally, our sense of touch connects us with everything we can see, hear, smell and taste. Thus, we might say that it is our most essential sense, for it is probably the most crucial for our survival—both physically and spiritually. Experts have shown time and again, for example, that touch for newborn infants and for babies is of primary importance to their physical and psychological development. They are touched, therefore they feel loved.

Adults also need to touch and be touched. We all need a warm handshake, a playful pat on the back, a nudge of encouragement, a stroke of support, a hug of closeness. We are all God's hands. It is through our sense of touch that we can heal and be healed by one another. Grace comes from God to us through our sense of touch in a very "tangible" way.

The Incarnation is the mystery of the physical connection between God and us. One of the results of classic asceticism, which tends to deny the value of our senses, has been the promotion of the idea that our bodies are somehow an obstacle to holiness. Jesus, however, never really promoted this type of spirituality. The ascetic practices that he asks for are closer to feasting than to fasting. His fasting is a fasting of the heart, much more than a fasting of the mouth. His discipline is that of service rather than isolation. His law is love of others, not ritual prescriptions.

Real saints have a sixth sense. They sense God in all of life's splendor, but they do so by using their other five senses. Spiritual life is merely ordinary life lived with God at its center. And when God is at the center, ordinary is ordinary no more. It is divine.

Thirteen

INTEGRITY

Everyone likes to talk about integrity, but not everyone likes to practice it. It is a peculiar quality, for we all claim to have it ourselves, but we tend to deny it in others. We expect integrity from our families, schools, churches, business and especially the government. Yet it seems more like a hope, a dream, a promise that never completely materializes.

Integrity, however, can be a spiritual path, if we can identify what exactly it is and how we might live lives filled with it. The dictionary associates integrity with "honesty," "uprightness of character," "soundness," "rectitude," "trustworthiness," "virtue," "adherence to a code of moral, artistic, or other values," "utter sincerity and candor," and the "state of being complete or undivided." Being complete or undivided means being a whole person, and the word "whole" comes from the same root as "holy." So being a person of integrity can mean being a holy person.

There are five important elements in the spirituality of integrity:

1. We must develop the ability to know ourselves in relationship to others and to God. This means that we not only are clear on our own deepest values and motivations but that we also understand the principles that regulate relationships. In other words, we have to be as worried about how our actions affect others and God as how they affect us.

2. We need to have the capacity to discern what is right and what is wrong. This is more than merely memorizing and following a list of laws and regulations. It means developing a highly sensitized conscience or "moral weather vane" that knows which way the moral wind is blowing, long before it is obvious.

3. We require the courage to say openly "yes" when we mean "yes," and "no" when we mean "no." This is no simple matter, for it implies first that we know where and for what we stand. It also means that we often tell people—even our loved ones, colleagues, or bosses—what they do not want to hear.

4. Once we have said "yes" or "no," we must have the daring to act according to what we have discerned and committed to—even at great personal cost. This

may include the loss of a relationship, the threat of financial insecurity or ruin, or even—in some extraordinary cases—physical threat or harm.

5. Finally, we need the determination to be holy—that is, whole and undivided. In our time, being holy is viewed as an unattainable and maybe even an unacceptable goal. But for those of us who wish to live lives of integrity, it is the only goal, one for which we can neither apologize nor be discouraged.

We need people of integrity who can help birth a world where truth is expected and reflected in every person.

Jesus was perhaps the most striking example of integrity the world has ever experienced. He lived according to what he knew to be his Father's will. He did not tolerate hypocrisy of any kind, even among his closest followers. He said what was on his mind without fear or calculation. He acted according to his convictions, even at great personal cost. He refused to compromise the truth.

Integrity can be a lonely spiritual path. Telling and living the truth can be uncomfortable, for it requires us to adjust to God's rules, not society's rules (or lack thereof). Truth also compels us to break our silence. Like Jesus, we have to speak up for what we believe to be just and good, for silence in this situation is an endorsement of wrongdoing.

Children can be our role models for integrity. Jesus said, "Whoever does not receive the kingdom of God as a little child will never enter it" (Luke 18:17). Children are—unless they have been corrupted by the adult world—genuine, innocent, simple, trusting. If they become phony and hypocritical, it is because the adult world trains them to be that way. It is their integrity that makes them close to God, not their naiveté.

Jesus asks every follower of his to carry the cross. He did not compromise his mission to political or financial or religious pressures. He was not in it for his personal gain or glory. All he wants is for us to live an authentic life of integrity, not a double life—one for God, the other for society.

One of the biggest tragedies of our time is the split between God and nature, spirit and matter, principle and practice. We need people of integrity who can help birth a world where truth is expected and reflected in every person. We need a spirituality of ordinary life in which there is no conflict between being a person of God and being a politician, business person, lawyer, actress, taxi driver or plumber.

⁂

Jesus was perhaps the most striking example of integrity the world has ever experienced.

⁂

Even though a life of integrity does not promise fame or wealth, sooner or later, it will be noticed and produce fruit. As Jesus taught: "Let your light shine before others, so that they may see your good works and give glory to your Father in heaven" (Matthew 5:16). Integrity, it seems, is a *sine qua non* of the kingdom of God.

Fourteen

PASSION

Sometimes we feel full of life, our energy overflowing with love and power. Other times we feel weak, depressed, bored, lonely and empty. The key is whether or not we are living lives of passion.

Zest for life is above all a choice that we make, but it is clear that living life to its fullest is an essential part of God's plan for us. "I came that they may have life, and have it abundantly" (John 10:10), Jesus said in explaining his mission. Saint Irenaeus has these inspiring words: "The glory of God is a human being who is fully alive."

We are fully alive when we use all our faculties, power, and talents, when we sharpen our physical and spiritual senses, when we are open to the complete potential of the human experience. Then we can allow ourselves to appreciate our feelings of wonder, compassion, tenderness, agony and ecstasy.

We are fully alive when we are thoughtful and reflective, when we ask the right questions, when we consider life to be a challenge to be lived rather than a matter of intellectual speculation. Our insights are reflected in our wills and hearts. Life is experienced not as a series of problems to be solved but as precious wine to be savored.

Zest for life is above all a choice that we make, but it is clear that living life to its fullest is an essential part of God's plan for us.

We are fully alive when we feel strongly that we belong to something bigger than ourselves—a family, a community, a church, a circle of friends, a professional group of people who work together for a certain cause. Isolation cannot define the person of passion. We are most who we are when we have a sense of belonging, when we have a palpable sense of "home." Aloofness does not fit well with being alive.

We are fully alive when we renew our faith in some kind of unity between ourselves and everybody and everything else around us. This immense work of the integration of all things is a work in progress. It is creating a higher level of consciousness that actually is generating a higher form of life—a life lived to all its dimensions. Only at this level of existence can real bonds of understanding and love be created among all beings. And only this kind of bonding will ensure a more compelling movement for human unity and peace.

When we believe that there is a direction to creation, that the entire universe is evolving in a direction, that we are all—each and every one of us—assigned an essential role in this immense enterprise, then boredom is out of the question. We know that our zest for life is going to make a difference in the world. We realize that we cannot afford to be less than passionate.

Some people cannot cope with passion. They are afraid to make mistakes or take risks. Alive people, on the other hand, are able to rely on love more than on laws, routines, customs, and mental calculations. Passion is a force that stimulates life, keeping it safe from stagnation and deterioration. When we are passionate, it is impossible to love less than "too much." Passion allows us to commit ourselves unconditionally to the values that ultimately lead us to union with God. When we dare to live with passion, the very act perforce leads to abandonment to the will of God.

Passion is not a theoretical concept. It is embodied in specific projects in each of our lives. These concrete projects are our contributions to the big project of existence, and our passion for our human projects is also a passion for the divine project. This is the meaning of the Incarnation. The Incarnation is the passion of God for us. It makes everything new and puts everything in perspective.

When we are passionate, it is impossible to love less than "too much."

Every time we express our creative passion, it pulls us closer to God. It allows us to lose any inclination we might have toward mediocrity in whatever we are and do. People of passion create music and art, discover new cures and inventions, explore uncharted territories. They fly higher and higher until they hear the words they most want to hear: "No one has ever done this before."

Fifteen

HOPE

Amid all of life's joys and sorrows, hope is constant. If we already are blessed with some measure of success and joy, we hope it continues. If illness and suffering are part of our destiny, we hope for relief and healing

Hope defines human nature. There certainly are times when life's worries and concerns and wants weigh heavily upon us and threaten to overwhelm us, but even then we continue to hope. Even our last breath carries with it the hope that it is not the end of life but merely a transition.

A few of us may try to live without faith or even love, but we cannot live without hope. If there is nothing to move us forward into the future, we lose interest in life itself. Specific expectations can be shattered, dreams can be destroyed, plans can be smashed, but hope must remain. We must be able to "hope against hope," or we will surely die—spiritually as well as physically.

Jesus' message of hope is not so much based on expectation of something yet to come but rather on the joy of something already present. He refused to work apocalyptic signs or strive to exercise political power. He wanted the improvement of society (which he most certainly desired) to be linked with his vision of the kingdom of God, which he said is already "among you" (Luke 17:21). Jesus never lost hope in his Father. His hope sprang from his communion with God. For him, instant fulfillment was not necessary. The only thing required was to have absolute trust in the goodness and love of God. Everything else would follow.

With hope there is always good news to be delivered, good deeds to be done, a good book to be read or written, a good friend to be cultivated.

Hope has its own particular angle among the virtues. It is the driving force that pulls the "not yet" into the "already here." Hope is not just wishful thinking, as in "I hope we have good weather tomorrow" or "I hope you will be the winner." It is, rather, a dynamic energy that carries us from the present into the future.

A sin against hope, then, is a sin against the Spirit. To despair is to deny that we are totally dependent on God or that our existence is that of pilgrims in an unknown land. Despair can be the most deceitful of attitudes. It means fleeing the battlefield of life and betraying life's deepest meaning. It leads to the conclusion that life is no longer worth living. And this is how evil, by stealing our most basic dream, declares its decisive victory.

⁂

Jesus' message of hope is not so much based on expectation of something yet to come but rather on the joy of something already present.

⁂

With hope there is always good news to be delivered, good deeds to be done, a good book to be read or written, a good friend to be cultivated. Hope is not a "what happens, happens" attitude. It is a state of constant anticipation, a "let's make it happen" outlook on life. With hope, we feel forever young and our possibilities are endless.

What makes life situations really difficult is the feeling that there is no escape. But hope always finds a way. "For God all things are possible" (Matthew 19:26), Jesus promised, and he was talking about hope. Hope is a divine gift that puts us in direct relationship with God:

> Those who wait for the LORD shall renew their strength,
>> they shall mount up with wings like eagles,
> they shall run and not be weary,
>> they shall walk and not faint.
>
> Isaiah 40:31

When we hope, we return to the very core of our being—the place where we are most at home—which is the state of "being with God." When we are in this place, we are immersed in a "holy insecurity"—a total reliance upon God that heals our self-doubt and distrust. By kneeling before God in hope, we learn to pray not only for our own daily bread but for the bread of all. We become instruments of the divine reality capable of bridging the gap between the world as it is and the world as God wants it to be.

ng on Baptism

bership first kindled?

mething special. What effect did it

There is nothing more satisfying than doing what we

are here on earth to do. Our inner call enables us to take stock of what really matters and frees us from clinging and clutter. There are several levels of call or *vocation* (a word derived from the Latin word for "call"). Our primary call is from God, and we all have the same one: to be a child of God. We also each have secondary calls to do specific work or go to specific places.

Since God has made us part of something bigger than ourselves, our inner call— which points to what God wants for each of us—is an overflowing source of energy in our lives.

There are ordinary secondary calls and special secondary calls. Very few people have a special call—a mission or job given to them through a direct communication from God. Most of us have an ordinary call, which is the life-task that we undertake in response to the primary call of Jesus: "Follow me" (Luke 9:23). We may call these secondary calls a career, an occupation, a job. They may include a state in life, such as being single or married, having children, or joining a religious order. These secondary vocations may change or end, but we can never retire from our primary vocation as followers of Christ.

Who among us does not have too many things to do? Just take a look at our calendars and schedules! When we have a sense of vocation, however, we can take a deep breath and begin to practice the presence of God in our busyness. We can put all things in perspective. A flood of fresh thoughts, emotions and inspirations will invade our being and force us to shift from our self-centeredness to God-centeredness. We will know that we are fulfilling the purpose of our life. We can begin to comprehend what we are here for.

When we find our true vocation, we also discover our true self. Our entire being becomes a "yes" to that call. A union of love blooms between us as the children of God and our Father. "Love" wrote Saint Therese of Lisieux in her autobiography, *Story of a Soul,* "is the vocation which includes all others." This call gives meaning to all that we do.

Since God has made us part of something bigger than ourselves, our inner call—which points to what God wants for each of us—is an overflowing source of energy in our lives. Following our vocation will make us fully alive...unless we get in the way.

ADDITIONAL RESOURCES

Grace Is Everywhere
Reflections of an Aspiring Monk
James Stephen Behrens, O.C.S.O.

Best-selling vignettes from the author's life at the Monastery of the Holy Spirit in Conyers, Georgia, with reflections on the connection between monastic spirituality and daily life. (160-page paperback, $9.95)

Pray with All Your Senses
Discovering the Wholeness Jesus Brings
Lo-Ann and David Trembly

A unique resource for both individual and group prayer. Focuses on how to use all five human senses along with a heightened sense of self to experience God more fully. Includes ten activities for exercising each sense in prayer. (124-page paperback, $8.95)

A Promise of Presence
Weekly Reflections and Daily Prayer Activities
Bridget Mary Meehan and Regina M. Oliver

Fifty-two reflections, each followed by a seven-day prayer guide, focusing on the intimate, personal relationship God seeks with each individual. Each reflection begins with a carefully chosen Scripture passage. (232-page paperback, $9.95)

**Available from booksellers or call 800-397-2282
in the U.S. or Canada.**